THE FRIENDLY GHOST

CASPER®

AND

HOT STUFF

SUPER SIZZLERS

tempo books
GROSSET & DUNLAP
A Filmways Company
Publishers • New York

CASPER AND HOT STUFF SUPER SIZZLERS

ISBN: 0-448-17095-7

A Tempo Books Original
Tempo Books is registered in the U.S. Patent Office

Published simultaneously in Canada
Printed in the United States of America

#9

THE FRIENDLY GHOST

CASPER®

AND

HOT STUFF

SUPER SIZZLERS

THE FRIENDLY GHOST
Casper®
IN
BOXCAR BAXTER
CATCH THIS TOUCHDOWN PASS, FATSO!
HA HA!

TALK ABOUT BUTTERFINGERS! IT WENT RIGHT THROUGH ALL THREE OF YOU! HA HA HA!

BIG DEAL! WHO CARES ABOUT FOOTBALL ANYWAY?

WELL, I DO! THROW ME A TOUCHDOWN PASS, CASPER!

GOOD CATCH!
THAT'S NOTHING!
THIS IS HOW YOU RUN THROUGH THE OTHER TEAM!
HEY!
TRY THAT AGAIN, DONKEY EARS!

BE ***CAREFUL***, HIPPITY!
OKAY!
WHAM!
NOW LET ***THAT*** BE A LESSON!

WHEN I WANT TO, I CAN BE AS SOLID AS A BRICK WALL!
BLAM!
HAW! SOME BRICK WALL!
OH, FATSO! YOU'D BETTER LIE DOWN!

LIE DOWN, CASPER? WHAT DO YOU THINK HE'S DOING NOW?
I MEAN IN A HAMMOCK, FUSSO!
I'LL MAKE SOME LEMONADE!
AND I THINK I'LL MAKE MYSELF SCARCE, CASPER!
HERE! I'VE MADE LEMONADE FOR EVERY-ONE, AND WE CAN WATCH THE FOOTBALL GAME!

FOR A NICE GUY, YOU SURE KNOW HOW TO RUB IT IN, CASPER!
EVERYBODY LOVES FOOTBALL, FATSO! LOOK! IT'S BOXCAR BAXTER!
HE'S THE ALL-STAR FULLBACK FOR THE PORCUPINES! HE'S A GIANT!

BIG DEAL!
HERE'S WHAT I THINK OF FOOTBALL!
POW!
OH!

W-WHAT *HIT* ME?
I DID!
HAW! SOME *GIANT,* CASPER!
WELL...THAT WAS A *LITTLE TV SET,* FATSO!

THE BIGGER THEY ARE, THE HARDER THEY FALL!
WHAM!
C'MON! PLAY BALL! WHO'S GOT THE BALL?

ER... I HAVE!
WOW! I KNOW THERE'S A SHORTAGE OF QUARTERBACKS, BUT...
FOLLOW ME!
BLAM!

TOUCHDOWN!

I'VE HAD ABOUT ENOUGH OF THIS!
US TOO!

HEY! WHAT STADIUM ARE WE IN?

I'VE NEVER BEEN BOOED IN MY LIFE!
I'M A STAR!

I HATE TO TELL YOU THIS, MR. BOXCAR, BUT THIS IS THE ENCHANTED FOREST AND THEY DON'T PLAY MUCH FOOTBALL AROUND HERE!!
THEN LET'S GET ORGANIZED! WE'LL WHIP UP A CHAMPIONSHIP TEAM IN NO TIME!

"NO TIME" IS RIGHT! THAT MEANS NEVER!

HEY! WHO TOLD YOU PRACTICE WAS OVER?!

NOBODY WALKS OUT ON BOXCAR!
IF YOU CAN GO THROUGH A WALL, SO CAN I!
CRASH!
?
NOW... LET'S SHAPE UP!
YOU HEARD THE LITTLE SQUIRT! UP!

WHERE ARE THEY GOING?
THEY'RE GOING UP! THEY DON'T LIKE FOOTBALL, MR. BOXCAR!
BUT EVERYBODY LOVES FOOTBALL!
ALMOST EVERYBODY!

LET'S FIND SOMEBODY ELSE TO PLAY WITH!
YOU CAN GET OUT OF SHAPE JUST STANDING AROUND!
FOLLOW ME, QUARTERBACK!
YOU KNOW, WE CAN HAVE A LITTLE FUN WITH THEM!
HOW?

BZZ BZZ BZZ BZ BZZ
HEH!
HEH!
ZZZZZZ
BETTER RUN, TROLL, OR YOU'LL BE SORRY!
SAYS WHO?
CASPER'S FOOTBALL FRIEND!

HIM? HA HA!
BLAM!
RUN, OGRE! HERE COMES CASPER'S FOOTBALL FRIEND!

HIM?
HAR HAR!

BLOOEY!

ISN'T THIS *FUN*, QUARTERBACK?
ER...

WE SHOULD BE REACHING THE GOAL LINE SOON!
OH, DEAR!
BOFF!
I SEE IT! I SEE THE GOAL POSTS!
OH, WAIT, BOXCAR! THAT'S...

... THE GATEWAY TO HORROR LAND..
ONLY ONE MAN BETWEEN US AND A TOUCHDOWN, QUARTERBACK!

WHOMP!

CASPER'S GOING TO GET IT NOW!
HA!
HA! HA!
HA! HA! HA!
OH, NO! D-DO YOU KNOW WHO THAT IS?

COME ON, QUARTERBACK! SCORE A TOUCHDOWN!

WE'VE ALREADY GOT A FIELD GOAL!
FOOLS!
HA HA HA
YOU LIKE FOOTBALL, DO YOU?
THAT'S THE WIZARD OF HORROR LAND!
SO BE IT!

WELCOME TO HORROR STADIUM! HAHAHAHA!

LOOK AT THESE CRAZY OUTFITS! I CAN HARDLY MOVE!
WHO'S THE OTHER TEAM? I CAN HARDLY WAIT!

HEH HEH! WAIT AND SEE! YOU'LL PAY FOR YOUR DISRESPECT!

WHAT ABOUT CASPER? HE SHOULD PAY, TOO!
YOUR FRIENDS ARE SWEET, CASPER!

I'VE HEARD OF CASPER THE SOFT-HEARTED! HIS PUNISHMENT WILL BE WATCHING YOU!

AND NOW... INTRODUCING THE TEAM FROM HORROR LAND!
AWK!
L-LET'S FLY OUT OF HERE!

I CAN'T! I DON'T SEEM TO HAVE ANY GHOSTLY POWERS AT ALL!

OKAY! HERE COMES OUR SAFETY MAN! PLAY BALL!

HEH HEH! WE'LL SEE HOW GOOD YOUR FRIENDS ARE, CASPER!

HAVEN'T I SEEN YOUR PLAYERS SOMEWHERE BEFORE
BOP!

BOF!
UGH!

TOUCHDOWN!
I FANCY YOU *HAVE* SEEN THEM BEFORE!
OOOF!
BONK

IF YOU WATCH HORROR MOVIES ON TV! SOME OF MY CREATURES ARE STARS!
OH!
HA HA! NOW LET'S WATCH YOUR LITTLE STAR, CASPER!
STOMP!

FUMBLE!

HA HA HA! IT'S A RUNAWAY!

SAY! YOUR LITTLE FRIEND IS SPUNKY!
SPLAT!

HE'S AN ALL STAR, MR. WIZARD! DIDN'T YOU EVER WATCH HIM ON TV?
NO! I WATCH ONLY HORROR MOVIES!
MAYBE I'VE BEEN MISSING SOMETHING!
CLICK!
AND THE PORCUPINES ARE LOSING AGAIN TODAY! NOBODY HAS BEEN ABLE TO FILL THE SHOES LEFT BEHIND AT LOCKER #12-- WHEN BOXCAR DISAPPEARED!

WHAT'S SO SPECIAL ABOUT THOSE SHOES? THEY'RE JUST BIG!
I'D LIKE TO SEE BOXCAR FILL THEM! HEH HEH!
OH, BOY! MY SECOND-HALF SHOES! WE CAN STILL WIN THIS GAME, TEAM!
WHAT GAME?

ZEEK!

FOLLOW OLD BOXCAR!

BLAM!
12
DID BOXCAR EVER FILL THOSE SHOES!
YAHOO!
BAM
SLAM!
12

OOF!
TOUCHDOWN!
NICE BLOCK, BOXCAR OLD PAL!
MY MONSTERS! HE'S RUINING MY MONSTERS!
AND FATSO SCORED A TOUCHDOWN!

WHO WANTS TO SEE BEAT-UP MONSTERS IN A HORROR MOVIE? ALL OF YOU, GO HOME!
I MUST HAVE BEEN ASLEEP! WHAT A CRAZY DREAM I HAD!
ME TOO! AND I'VE GOT THE BUMPS TO PROVE IT!

LET'S GO LOOK AT THE TV SET UPSTAIRS! THERE'S SOMETHING I WANT TO SEE!

BOXCAR BAXTER IS BACK, FOLKS! AND SCORING!
12

FUNNY...I NEVER CARED MUCH ABOUT FOOTBALL BEFORE!
12
I GUESS IT'S DIFFERENT WHEN YOU'RE WATCHING AN OLD TEAMMATE!
THE END

HOT STUFF®
THE LITTLE DEVIL
IN The Little Lost ICICLE
WHAT A DAY! THE SUN IS SHINING, THE BIRDS ARE CHIRPING, THE BROOK IS BABBLING- AND SOMEONE'S SOBBING!
SOB! SOB!

SOBBING?!
A LIVING ICICLE!! WHAT'S THE TROUBLE?
ALL THE OTHER ICICLES ARE GONE...
HA!
ISN'T IT GREAT?! THE WEATHER IS SO NICE!
BAW! I WANT MY MOMMA AND POPPA!

THEY'LL REWARD YOU IF YOU TAKE ME HOME!
OKAY, KID! I'LL GET MY ASBESTOS GLOVE, SO I DON'T MELT YOU!
AFTER A WHILE..
G-GOSH! IT'S COLD AROUND HERE!
THE NORTH POLE IS JUST AROUND THE BEND!

SOON!
HI, MA! HI, PA! I'M BACK.!!
OUR LITTLE FRIDGY HAS RETURNED!!
WHO'S THAT WITH YOU?
THAT'S HOT STUFF! HE SAVED ME!

HE DID?!
BUT DEVILS DON'T LIKE ICICLES!
I SAID YOU'D REWARD HIM!
A PROMISE IS A PROMISE! GO HOME AND WAIT FOR YOUR REWARD!
THANKS! 'BYE!
MAYBE I'LL GET A BEARSKIN COAT!
OR A BUSHEL OF APPLES—

OR MAYBE A LIFETIME SUPPLY OF FROZEN CUSTARD...
LATER, BACK IN THE CAVE...
I CAN HARDLY WAIT FOR MY REWARD!
NEXT MORNING...
BRRR IT'S C-C-COLD!!

HI, THERE! AS YOUR REWARD WE'VE DECIDED YOU'LL HAVE AIR CONDITIONING ALL YEAR 'ROUND!

I APPRECIATE THAT, BUT IT WON'T BE NECESSARY! I PREFER IT NICE AND WARM!
YOU GOT IT COMING AND YOU'LL TAKE AIR CONDITIONING, LIKE IT OR NOT!

THANKS, BUT NO THANKS!!
SO SCRAM!

HEY! THAT'S HOT!

LET'S GET HIM AND FREEZE HIM FOR KEEPS!
UH-OH!
THE UNGRATEFUL DEVIL!!

THEY CAN'T GET WHAT THEY CAN'T SEE... IT'S INVISIBLE TIME!
POOF!
TRY GRABBING THIS INSTEAD!!

STRIKE!

SUDDENLY...
WHA-? THEY'VE MELTED INTO A SHEET OF ICE!
RIGHT ON MY FLOOR!
IT'S SO COLD IN THERE, IT WON'T THAW FOR WEEKS!
AND IF I MELT IT, IT'LL FLOOD MY CAVE!
TSK!

IDEA!
HOT STUFF'S ICE SKATING RINK
ADMISSION 5 APPLES
I GOT MY REWARD AFTER ALL!
TICKETS
THE END

HOT STUFF®
THE LITTLE DEVIL
IN
DR. STRANGE-EYES
HA!
THAT'S FUNNY!
ROAR!!
EEK!

A MOUSE CHASING A CAT!?
RAT RAT TAT!
YOW!
A WOODPECKER... RAPPING ON STONE??
RAT TAT
TAT!

WELL, NOW I'VE SEEN EVERYTHING!
HA! I WON'T SEE ANYTHING LIKE THAT AGAIN 'TIL THE PIGS BEGIN TO FLY!!
EE-YOW!

CHOINK!
CHOINK!
S-SOMETHING WEIRD IS G-GOING ON!
PIGS HAVE BEGUN TO FLY!
WHAT COULD BE HAPPENING??
HA HA HA!

YI! W-WHO'S LAUGHING?!!
ONLY ME! HA-HA!

WHO ARE YOU?
I AM DOCTOR STRANGE-EYES! MAGICIAN EXTRAORDINARY —AT YOUR SERVICE!

THEN YOU MUST BE MAKING ALL THOSE STRANGE THINGS HAPPEN!
OH- HA-HA! YOU NOTICED MY LITTLE TRICKS!!

I HOPE YOU ENJOYED THEM...
THEY ARE HARMLESS!

YES—COME TO THINK OF IT, THEY ARE FUN! HA HA!
WOULD YOU CARE TO SEE MORE?
IN FACT—HOW WOULD YOU LIKE TO HELP ME WITH MY FAVORITE TRICK?
SURE!
NOW JUST LOOK RIGHT INTO MY EYES!
OKAY!

HA! YOU ARE NOW IN MY POWER! YOU WILL DO EXACTLY AS I SAY!

WE WILL GO TO MY HIDEOUT!
SAY 'YES, MASTER'!
YES, MASTER!!

SOON..
AND NOW I WILL GIVE YOU YOUR FIRST ASSIGNMENT!

YOU WILL GO OUT INTO THE ENCHANTED FOREST AND TAKE CANDY FROM A BABY!
THIS IS TO TEST YOU FOR BIGGER THINGS!
YES, MASTER!

—AND DO NOT RETURN WITHOUT THAT CANDY!
YES, MASTER!

NOT FAR AWAY...
GOO-GOO!*
* YUM-YUM!
URG!!!*
*WHAT'S UP??

G-GOLLY! WHAT'S GOT INTO HOT STUFF?
BAW!*
*BAW!
SO! YOU HAVE COMPLETED YOUR FIRST ASSIGNMENT!
YES, MASTER!
WELL DONE! YOU MAY GO INSIDE!

YOU ARE NOW READY FOR THE BIG JOB- OPERATION "G"!!
LICK LICK!

OPERATION "G", MASTER??

YES! YOU WILL NOW STEAL ALL THE GOLD FROM FORT KNOCK!!
YES, MASTER!

AND DON'T COME BACK WITHOUT THAT GOLD!
YES, MASTER!

FORT
KNOCK

HERE COMES
HOT STUFF!
HI!
FORT KNOCK
GOLD SUPPLY

HA!
YOW!
SASS!
OW!

W-WHAT'S GOT INTO HOT STUFF?
I SEE IT, BUT I DON'T BELIEVE IT!
FORT KNOCK
GOLD SUPPLY
14K
14K
14K
SASSs

HISSSS!
H-HE MELTED THE INGOTS INTO A RIVER OF GOLD! —AND HE'S MAKING IT FLOW DOWNHILL!

H-HE'S KEEPING IT FLOWING WITH *HOT FORK BLASTS!!*
WITHOUT THAT GOLD, PETER THE PAINTER WON'T BE ABLE TO PAINT THE *GOLDEN FLOWERS* AND *BIRDS!*

HI, FELLAS! I'M HERE TO GET GOLD FOR MY PAINT!
PETER! SOMETHING *AWFUL* HAS HAPPENED!

HOT STUFF HAS STOLEN ALL THE GOLD!
W-WHAT?
THE GOLDFINCHES AND GOLDENRODS AND BUTTERCUPS ALL NEED GOLD PAINTING!!
I'LL FOLLOW THIS TRAIL WHILE IT'S STILL HOT...
...AND SEE IF I CAN GET TO THE BOTTOM OF THIS!

SO THIS IS WHERE THE GOLD FLOWED!- BUT WHY DID HOT STUFF STEAL IT??
IT'S NOT LIKE HIM AT ALL!
HMM... THE GOLD GOES INTO THAT CELLAR!
YIKES!
HOT STUFF IS SAWING IT INTO GOLD INGOTS WITH HIS TRIDENT FIRE!
SSS

HA!
-ALL THE GOLD IN FORT KNOCK! I'M RICH-- RICH! DO YOU HEAR?
-BUT NOT RICH ENOUGH! I WANT MORE-AND YOU WILL STEAL IT FOR ME! LOOK INTO MY EYES!
SO THAT'S IT! HOT STUFF IS HYPNOTIZED!

YES, MASTER!!
HA HA!
MORE! MORE! MORE AND MORE!!
WHOOPS! MY GLASSES!
I CAN'T SEE WITHOUT MY GLASSES!!

BESIDES...
...I CAN'T KEEP HOT STUFF HYPNOTIZED WITHOUT THEM EITHER!
CRA-ACK!!
BAW! I BROKE MY GLASSES! MY POWER IS GONE!
W-WHERE AM I?

HOT STUFF! YOU WERE HYPNOTIZED! THE SPELL IS BROKEN!
I HEAR VOICES! I MUST ESCAPE!
CRASH!!
THAT FIEND HYPNOTIZED YOU AND MADE YOU MELT THE GOLD IN FORT KNOCK SO IT WOULD FLOW DOWN TO THIS CELLAR!
AND HE ALSO HAD YOU STEAL CANDY FROM A BABY!

WE MUST GET THE GOLD BACK AS SOON AS POSSIBLE! THE GOLDENROD AND GOLDFINCHES AND EVERYTHING ELSE THAT'S GOLDEN NEEDS PAINTING!
DON'T WORRY, PETER! I'LL SEE THAT IT'S ALL RETURNED!
SO...LATER...
HOW'S IT GOING, PETER?
FINE! JUST FINE, HOT STUFF!
WE COULDN'T GET THE GOLD TO FLOW BACK UPHILL BUT WE'RE GETTING IT UP HERE ANYWAY!
NOW THAT'S THE OLD HOT STUFF!
GOO!
THE END

HOT STUFF®
THE LITTLE DEVIL
BE GENTLE WITH PERCY, HOT STUFF, HE'S ONLY A CHILD!
OKAY, AUNTIE CLINKER!

WHAT AUNTIE CLINKER DOESN'T KNOW...
...IS THAT LITTLE PERCY HERE, IS A *BRAT*...
OF THE *FIRST* ORDER!

HA!
OW!
SASS!

HAW!
GIVE ME THAT TRIDENT, YOU LITTLE RASCAL!

WHAT HE DOESN'T KNOW...
IS THAT THE VERY NEXT TIME HE PULLS A FAST ONE ON ME...

LATER-
HA! HA!
HUH?? MY FORK! THE HEAT CAN'T GET OUT!
THE KNOT IS JAMMIN' IT!

...HIS LITTLE PLAN WILL BACKFIRE!!
POW
OW!
THE END

HOT STUFF®
THE LITTLE DEVIL
IN
BANG LAND
BOY, I'M BORED!
SAY! THAT CHARACTER LOOKS LIKE HE NEEDS EXCITEMENT!
THIS CRACKER WILL GIVE HIM A LIFT!

I'M EVEN HEARING SIZZLING SOUNDS!
PWANG!
FLOPP!!

BANG-
LAND

I DON'T KNOW WHERE I AM?
BUT AN EXPLOSION GOT ME HERE!

THE ONLY CLUE I HAVE IS THIS CRUMMY SIGN!
BANG-LAND

BANG!

THAT S-STARTLED ME!
I HATE SUDDEN B-BANGS!

I'M GETTING OUT OF HERE!
THIS PLACE IS CREEPY!!
I'M CERTAINLY NOT GETTING A BANG OUT OF BANGLAND!
BANG!

STUPID BALLOON!

BANG!
BANG!
POW!

M-MORE B-BALLOONS!
I'D BETTER LOOK FOR THE EXIT!
MAYBE I'LL HAVE ME ONE OF THESE COCONUTS FOR REFRESHMENT!

CRACK!
CRACK!
TH-THOSE NUTS COULDN'T STAND MY BODY HEAT!
A CORNFIELD... WHAT HARM COULD COME TO ME HERE?

POP
POP
POP
POP
POP
POP
POP
IT WOULD HAVE TO BE POPCORN!

ALL THESE BANGS AND POPS ARE *WEARING* ME *DOWN!*

I GUESS THIS OLD LOG IS A GOOD PLACE TO REST!
I GUESS I GUESSED WRONG!!
VROOOOM!

BAM!
BOOM!

BANG!

AT LEAST THAT LAST BANG WAS USEFUL!
HOWL! IT'S THAT SAME CHARACTER WE BLASTED! LET'S KEEP AWAY FROM HIM!
OW
THE END

THE FRIENDLY GHOST
Casper®
IN
GO FETCH!
WHERE ARE YOU GOING, FATSO?
TO FEED SPOOCH, CASPER!
SPOOC

HOW NICE!
DON'T BE A SIMP!
HE JUST FEEDS YOUR DOG SO HE WON'T COME AROUND THE TABLE BEGGING WHEN WE EAT!
POOCH
RIGHT! YOU KNOW HOW THAT BIG MUTT LOVES GHOST MULLIGAN STEW!

DON'T UNCOVER THAT UNTIL I LOCK THE DOOR AND WINDOWS!
OKAY!
AHHH... SMELL THAT!
SNIFF SNIFF!

THUNK!

WARF! WARF!

BEAT IT!

GET LOST!

SLURP!
DOGGONE IT, SPOOCH! WHEN WILL YOU LEARN TO BE A REAL DOG?
YOU'VE HURT HIS FEELINGS, FATSO!

YOU KNOW SPOOCH WANTS TO BE A REAL DOG MORE THAN ANYTHING ELSE!
WELL...REAL DOGS DON'T FLY THROUGH WALLS AND BEG THROUGH THE TABLETOP!
THEY CHASE THE MAILMAN AND FETCH YOUR SLIPPERS AND...
WARF! WARF!

HEH HEH! I GOT RID OF HIM!
FATSO! HOW MEAN!
SENDING SPOOCH ON A WILD-GOOSE CHASE! MAILMEN ARE AFRAID TO COME NEAR GHOSTS!
AND NOBODY AROUND HERE EVEN WEARS SLIPPERS!

SPOOCH?
SPOOCH!

WARF!
SPOOCH! HERE, BOY!

WOW! WHERE DID YOU FIND THAT?

THAT'S THE BIGGEST SLIPPER I EVER SAW!
SIZE G14

WHERE DID YOU GET IT, SPOOCH?

WAS IT A GIANT SIGN FOR A SHOE STORE?
NO... I GUESS NOT! IT'S BEEN WORN!
WORN?
SPOOCH! WHERE DID YOU...

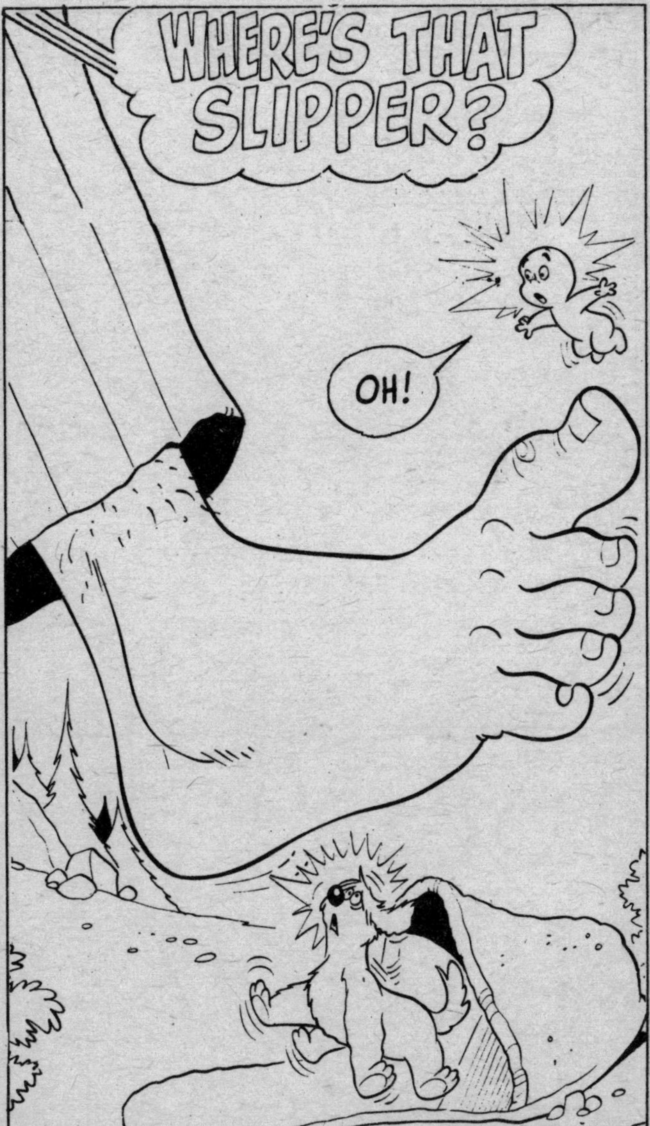
WHERE'S THAT SLIPPER?
OH!

GRMPH! HOW CAN A SLIPPER WALK AWAY BY ITSELF?
WOW! THAT'S THE BIGGEST GIANT I'VE EVER SEEN!

HIS HEAD IS IN THE CLOUDS!
LOOK OUT, SPOOCH! HERE COMES HIS FOOT!
...AND HERE COMES HIS OTHER FOOT... RIGHT AT OUR HOUSE!

I NEVER TRIED TO STEER A BIG TOE BEFORE!
WHEW! CLOSE!
UH-OH... NOW HE'S COMING DOWN ON A WHOLE ELF VILLAGE!

SPOOCH! HELP ME!
DON'T JUST FLOAT THERE! HELP ME!
?
SLURP!

HEE HEE
THAT TICKLED!
I REALLY NEED MY SLIPPER!
WARF!

WELL... AREN'T YOU A NICE LITTLE DOG!

COME HOME WITH ME!

SPOOCH!

I'LL TEACH YOU TO SIT AT MY FEET AND WALK WITH ME! I HOPE YOU CAN TAKE GIANT STEPS!

MR. GIANT... SPOOCH IS MY DOG! KOFF KOFF!

KOFF KOFF!
THESE AREN'T CLOUDS AT ALL! IT'S PIPE SMOKE!

NOW THESE ARE REAL CLOUDS!
NO WONDER I NEVER KNEW THERE WAS A GIANT'S CASTLE UP HERE!
OH, GOLLY! HOW NICE THEY LOOK TOGETHER!

I GUESS SNIFF! SPOOCH LIKES THE GIANT MORE THAN ME!
I KNOW HE'LL BE HAPPY! THAT'S A NICE GIANT!
AH... THIS IS PEACEFUL... ZZZZ

ZZZZZZ
WARF!
SPOOCH!
WHERE'S MY LITTLE DOG?

I GUESS I WAS DREAMING!
BUT I THINK I WILL GET A DOG OF MY OWN! IT'S A NICE FEELING!
IT IS A NICE FEELING, SPOOCH!

AND YOU WERE REALLY NICE TO MAKE THE GIANT FEEL GOOD!
LOOK! FATSO LEFT SOME OF HIS GHOSTLY MULLIGAN STEW!
ENJOY IT! I HAVE A FEELING YOU'LL TRAIN US ALL SOON!
THE END